REI
HUMILITY

REIGNING IN HUMILITY

CARRIE PICKETT

Published in partnership between Andrew Wommack Ministries and Harrison House Publishers

Shippensburg, PA 17257

ISBN 13 TP: 978-1-6675-0471-1

ISBN 13 eBook: 978-1-6675-0472-8

For Worldwide Distribution, Printed in the U.S.A.

1 2 3 4 5 6 7 8 / 27 26 25 24 23

Dedication

May you discover the incredible realm of "more grace" that only God can supply when you live in humility!

Contents

Introduction 9

Switching Kingdoms 12

God is God 15

Your Value System 17

Obedience 20

The Fear of the Lord 22

Pride: The Enemy of Humility 24

Pride: The Champion of Fear 27

Pride Follows Its Own Path 30

Humility and Our Call 32

Lead with a Servant's Heart 34

Finding God's Will 36

Staying Humble in God's Will 38

Humility and Integrity 40

Humility and Patience 42

God is a Jealous God....................................44
Humility and Behavior 46
Humility in Action..48
Humility and Persecution 50
Humility to Remain Steadfast 53
Humility and Promotion 55
Conclusion 58

Introduction

"...If anyone would come after me, let him deny himself and take up his cross..."

Matthew 16:24

We've read or heard this verse many times, but is denying ourselves part of our heart's motivation?

Now, denial is not about living our lives with heads lowered because we're wired with a meek personality. Denying oneself is a posture of humility. Humility is pushed aside anytime we obsess over our abilities or focus on personal shortcomings. The world constantly tells us to rise, to become, to attain. When we've allowed *self* to become our preoccupation, it's tempting to look down on ourselves or on others based on where we have or have not arrived. Measuring ourselves against anything other than God's

Word affects our Christian walk and promotes pride in our hearts.

Humility is acknowledging the God we said *yes* to and surrendering our personalities, our giftings, and our circumstances to the Lordship of Jesus. It's taking our position as His child and stewarding what we have in Christ. If we're not postured in humility, we cannot truly lead, make an impact, or be entrusted with anything. Self will demand its way, find an excuse, or pursue a distraction. Abiding in humility is a place where God is able to exert His power and divine influence in and through us.

I'm going to be bold in this study because so many of you have been spinning your wheels in your own strength and in pride. You want to be used mightily; but spinning wheels without any traction will get you stuck in the same groove.

Allow Jesus to be your example throughout this booklet. You'll see demonstrations of a humbled posture—one that involves tenderness, but also courage and total dependence on God. You will be able to identify areas where you've leaned on your own understanding instead of surrendering to the One with all the answers.

This is your season to get unstuck. A steadfast motivation to remain humble is not far from you. Humbly seek His help to stay under His guardianship. You'll find that humility brings honor, promotion, and allows you to move forward in the destiny God has for you.

Carrie G. Pickett

Switching Kingdoms

Your first step toward reigning in humility began when you asked Jesus to become your Savior. Repentance delivered you from Satan's domain and transferred you into God's kingdom; and you entered it totally forgiven, completely cleansed (1 Jn. 1:9).

Once you switched kingdoms, the Spirit of God came to dwell within you. His Spirit makes reigning possible because you carry all the attributes and character of God. You're now a threat to Satan because he knows what you possess and works tirelessly to keep you from acknowledging what is yours. He does this by attempting to shift your focus away from Jesus and God's Word.

John 1:12 reads: *But to all who did receive him, who believed in his name, he gave the right to become children of God.* Part of reigning in humility is knowing that as God's child, you are of the same glorious seed! As Jesus is, so are you in this world (1 Jn. 4:17). Jesus' life provided a template of what you possess: truth, righteousness, power, authority, **humility**, and more. He stood apart from the world by choosing to depend on God.

As God's child, you are of the same glorious seed!

You have the same choice. Philippians 2:8 says that Jesus humbled Himself and was obedient to the point of death. This shows Christ's courage. He didn't waver in His decision to suffer crucifixion; He knew His purpose. Thank God that you don't have to die for anyone's salvation; but this same courage reigns inside of you! You only access this kind of courage when your confidence rests on all you've inherited. Knowing your inheritance and how to best steward it comes by way of relationship and remaining in the Word.

You may have applied pieces of your inheritance to some areas of your life but have left others untouched, namely humility. You've allowed the enemy, your senses, or your intellect to mess with your focus. The quickest fix is easy:

repent! Go back to the joy of your salvation and remember whose kingdom you belong to.

God is God

Every attribute Jesus demonstrated was founded on humility. Jesus told His disciples, *"I tell you the truth, the Son can do nothing by himself. He does only what he sees the Father doing"* (Jn. 5:19 NLT).

What do *you* see the Father doing? You see the Father in the life of Jesus. He is your example and you're called to live your life for God. Settle in your heart that God is God—He is the way, the truth, and the life (Jn. 14:6). It is foolishness for Christians to live life apart from God's leading and expect Him to bless it. He will not share His glory. You've been blessed with talents and abilities but they're not meant to highlight you. God wants to shine *through* them for His glory.

Exemplifying humility means you're teachable. Jesus said, *"Take my yoke upon you, and learn from me, for I am gentle and lowly in heart, ... For my yoke is easy and my burden is light"* (Matt. 11:29-30). If you've allowed religion,

When you exalt God above anything you can do alone, you mirror the heart of Jesus. You reflect the heartbeat of humility.

the world, or yourself to be your teacher, you're probably stuck in pride. If you'll humble yourself, seek His face, do a one-eighty, God will hear and heal you (2 Chron. 7:14). It takes humility to run to God and tell Him that He hasn't been a priority. God won't condemn but help you and reveal the destiny you should've been pursuing all along.

Part of that destiny is being an extension of Jesus' mission to destroy the works of the devil (1 Jn. 3:8). The role you have in the kingdom is vital. You have the privilege to present the total package of Christ—His nature and character—in ways that counter misconceptions others may have. When you humble yourself and ask the Lord, *"How can I reveal You today?"* you have the potential to bring others to the saving knowledge of Christ. You can change the course of a family, a marriage, a friendship.

When you exalt God above anything you can do alone, you mirror the heart of Jesus. You reflect the heartbeat of humility.

Your Value System

I believe that you don't want to stay at the level you're at. You want to be a reflection of Christ but don't see God's abundance flowing from you. The enemy knows what keeps you from walking in the fullness of your salvation. The question is, do you?

Paul, the self-proclaimed "Pharisee of Pharisees," was groomed from birth to later land high positions of knowledge and status. Who better to persecute the church than someone obsessed with rank and credentials? His pride was ripe for the devil's use.

However, Paul's destiny changed the moment he encountered Jesus. In Galatians 2:20, Paul said that he was crucified with Christ. This is huge! Whatever Paul valued—his lineage, his knowledge of the law, his position—all died. Similarly in Philippians 3:8, Paul considered those

> **It takes faith to stand against wordly ideals and a humble heart to only care what God thinks.**

things as loss compared to the surpassing worth of knowing and gaining Christ. Not just those things, but all things.

Paul's value system changed. Nothing was more worthy than growing in Christ and letting truth transform his identity. When you encountered Christ, was there a change in your value system? What areas in your life seem to provide an edge? Do you place value on past successes or failures? These questions warrant serious consideration because if what you value supersedes God's Word, you're letting them have authority; you're letting them hinder or dictate the direction of your life. When they "speak," faith and humility suffer.

Faith and humility operate in tandem. When you say you believe God's Word, that's faith. Yet, it simultaneously takes humility to push aside the things that seem to offer an advantage: education, status, finances. Others might think you're crazy for not applying natural resources; but it takes faith to stand against worldly ideals and a humble heart to only care what God thinks.

Life isn't about your righteousness or worldly standards. Press toward the goal for the prize of the upward call of God (Phil. 3:14). Value Him and His abundance and His impact will begin to flow from you.

Obedience

The zeal that Paul had to persecute the church was the same zeal he later used to stay humble—to keep values in their proper place. *The reward for humility and fear of the Lord is riches and honor and life* (Prov. 22:4). Humility and fear refer to reverencing God; it's the value that's placed on Him and obedience to His Word. If there's only one God, why do some believers seem to value and serve everything else?

Our culture tells us to make a mark in this world—to influence by promoting what we do. Making a mark and influencing depends on whose name is receiving the honor. *One's pride will bring him low, but he who is lowly in spirit will obtain honor* (Prov. 29:23). God can promote us to positions of influence and people may know our name, but we aren't meant to seek honor for ourselves. *Pride goes before destruction, a haughty spirit before a fall* (Prov. 16:18).

A life marked by humility and obedience is a life God honors. When I see my kids humble themselves by sacrificing time or things for others, my heart is moved. They weren't focused on themselves. Their motivation stemmed from obedience.

Obedience is an attribute of humility.

Obedience is an attribute of humility. Obedience comes from a heart that says, *"No matter what, I am going to trust You, Lord."* I remember teaching at a conference and the Lord told me to sing in tongues...and then sing the interpretation! Self-consciousness consumed me and I gulped, *"Are You sure, Lord?"* But I had determined long ago that whatever He says, I will do. This wasn't about me. So, I sang and gave the interpretation. I cannot tell you just how powerful the move of God was in that place.

Don't put value on your abilities, inabilities, or how the world might respond. Let your zeal be after the God that you love and serve. You can't let pride or disobedience keep you from being used by God to touch the lives of others.

The Fear of the Lord

In 1 Corinthians 11:1, Paul tells the church to follow him as he followed Christ. How could Paul make such a bold statement? Paul reigned in humility. Humility taught him that everything belonged to God. That's why Paul counted all he gained as loss; that's why he considered his life crucified with Christ. Paul's fear (reverence) of God was the beginning of wisdom. Following God's commandments gave Paul an inroad to understanding (Ps. 111:10).

Fear of the Lord isn't about performance, avoiding punishment, or thinking God will smite you with something terrible because you've sinned. Sin has consequences; but reverencing God is submitted and joyful abandonment to God's sovereignty. Sovereignty is revealed in God's grandeur—His might, power, justice, and holiness. Yet in all of that greatness, God wants an intimate relationship with you! That was the game-changer for Paul. Living for God wasn't about his knowledge or status, or what he did for God. It was about relationship; it was about fully understanding God's true nature, character, and prioritizing God's values and standards above his own.

> Humility is a place where you begin to live your life with God's perspective.

Paul said that when others followed his example of living, the God of peace would be with them (Phil. 4:9). God used Paul's life as he followed after Christ's humility, Christ's obedience, Christ's reverence for God.

Humility is the place where you begin to live your life with God's perspective. There's no *you* in the equation. Following God's precepts brings a peace and a zeal to want to know more.

When you understand that God—in all His grandeur—lives inside of you and wants His best for you, you'll easily identify the schemes of the devil. You'll not only shun evil, but God will promote you to a position of authority and influence that will lead others to turn from their evil ways. The fear and humility you submit yourself to is a lifestyle of obedience that honors God. In turn, He blesses you with riches, honor, and life!

Pride: The Enemy of Humility

I've alluded to pride in terms of self-focus, self-reliance, and self-promotion. A closer examination of our hearts may reveal other manifestations of pride: fear, worry, anxiety, offense, resentment, doubt. The bottom line is that pride is the enemy of humility. Pride reveals a heart that isn't clothed in humility and creates a barrier to truly loving God more than ourselves.

A fear of the Lord is essential to wisdom; a teachable heart is essential to the counsel of God. In John 14:26, the Holy Spirit is called the Counselor who *teaches* all things. Many of us are guilty of only seeing Him as a consultant. Consultants offer advice and share their expertise. God is not a consultant. He teaches truth. However, we decide if we are going to line up our motives with truth. Stubbornly going with *our* inner consult rather than trusting

God is pride. Even when we do acknowledge truth, we still may turn that on ourselves: *Gee, what kind of Christian am I? God, how could You use someone like me?* False humility is also pride. God loves and never forsakes us, but God cannot bless pride.

Pride reveals a heart that isn't clothed in humility and creates a barrier to truly loving God more than ourselves.

Humility casts all cares upon God (1 Pet. 5:7). However, people tend to cast cares like casting a fishing line. Their "lure" (debt, illness, family problem, etc.) is cast in prayer hoping God will "bite." While waiting, time has allowed all the *what ifs* to surface, or the ways God *could* answer. In the end, people reel in the line, take ownership of their concerns, and struggle for their own solutions. *Many are the plans in the mind of a man, but it is the purpose of the Lord that will stand* (Prov. 19:21). Man's pride leads to destruction (Prov 19:3).

Thinking that we have the right plans and strategies usually leaves us depleted and frustrated because we're doing things in our own strength. We have a Counselor who is always with us, the very Spirit of God willing to bring revelation. Let us endeavor to be led with a humble, teachable spirit.

Pride: The Champion of Fear

Pride brings so many negative emotions. I've already highlighted some, but I want to focus on fear. Fear can be overwhelming because we've been conditioned to respond to our senses. The things that elicit fear mask themselves: *How can you ignore this? You should be very concerned. Think of your family, your future!*

Fear, like any manifestation of pride, happens when we take our eyes off God. When we're not immersed in truth, we're vulnerable to the enemy: *You can't break this habit; you won't amount to anything. This is hereditary; what makes you think it won't attack you?* If we place value on comments like these, fear can rise. We then exalt fear by being fixated on scenarios we've imagined. Then we bring those possibilities into our conversations with others who

> Humility produces a fruit of authority to speak against fear, to speak life, and to prophesy God's unchanging faithfulness into our future.

give credence to our fear. In time, fears become full-blown cares that exalt themselves above God.

However, according to Isaiah 54:14, fear doesn't have a chance! *In righteousness you shall be established; you shall be far from oppression, for you shall not fear; and from terror, for it shall not come near you.* Anytime we've allowed pride to reign as fear, repentance is in order. We need to humble ourselves to the Word and His counsel and ask, *"Lord, what do you want me to do?"* We find the answer in Isaiah 41:10: *...fear not, for I am with you; be not dismayed, for I am your God; I will strengthen you, I will help you, I will uphold you with my righteous right hand.*

Recently, God showed me that I placed pressure on myself to guide my daughter through some attitudes and to help her love God above all else. My guidance, though, was more like "fixing", and I was hard on my daughter in the process. I had taken my eyes off God and took ownership of my concerns. My efforts were out of love; but when

I placed her in His care, God reminded me that He would bring the harvest.

We have the choice to fear or to be humble. Humility produces a fruit of authority to speak against fear, to speak life, and prophesy God's unchanging faithfulness to our future.

Pride Follows Its Own Path

Pride cannot lay an adequate future. Plans may seem doable, but pride paves the way for pitfalls: the enemy's lies and all negative emotions. Pride relies on its own knowledge and timelines rather than truth and divine guidance. Again, God cannot bless pride; He actually resists the proud! But in His infinite mercy, God gives grace to the humble (1 Pet. 5:5).

Proverbs 16:17 says that "*the highway of the upright is to depart from evil.*" Only the humble make it their aim to avoid wickedness—they don't even invite it! They've prioritized relationship with God to guard themselves from being taken captive by the world's philosophies (Col. 2:8). The world is never short on its delivery. Many things entice us to go after what we want, to have it when we want it, and to enjoy it how we want to. If we stay self-centered and push aside God's influence and timing, we'll land on the broad path that leads to destruction (Matt. 7:13).

When pride comes, shame and disgrace follow; but with humility is wisdom (Prov. 11:2). There are things in our lives that came to naught—things our hearts should have never pursued, places we were never destined to go. Humility invites us to higher levels of wisdom and maturity.

Humility is a lifestyle of intimacy lavished in God's grace.

Both wisdom and maturity tell us that it's better to be of a lowly spirit than to divide the spoils with the proud (Prov 16:19). This is the same lowly spirit of Christ—a heart surrendered to the heart of God. When we are surrendered, we won't participate in the same selfishness, ambitions, and mindsets of the proud.

Humility is a lifestyle of intimacy lavished in God's grace. God must be our hiding place and His Word our source of hope (Ps. 119:114). Life cannot be navigated following our own path determined with our purposes. Anything built on self will fall (Prov. 16:18).

Humility and Our Call

The heart of humility is found in a believer who knows their call. This is not just for the super saint; it's for the one who has been chiseled and taught by trials—the soul that has gained wisdom to say, *"Lord, no matter what life has dealt, no matter the world's opinions, I know You've chosen me and have something better!"* God is a show-off, meaning that He wants to shine brightly in us. Our lives are to exemplify God's magnificence so that others see a visible demonstration of an invisible God.

The key to overflow with God's goodness isn't being the best of the best. God chooses the weak and humble to reveal His power and glory (1 Cor. 1:26). Christians may understand that God chose them but see nothing spectacular within themselves. But humility is what makes us great candidates for the spectacular! A humbled heart surrenders everything that appears to disqualify *or even qualify* us for God's use.

We saw this in Paul's life. By the world's standards, he was qualification personified. Yet after he was called, he regarded his former life as nothing. His only determination was to know Christ and Him crucified (1 Cor. 2:2). The more we prioritize knowing God, advantages and disadvantages get swallowed up in relationship! God is then able to move powerfully in our lives.

My husband Mike tells the story of one of his friends who was fired from a job. Instead of focusing on the loss, Mike's friend humbly asked God for his next steps. As he stayed close to God, God showed him how to use his talents to create useful inventions. He was then able to sell them regularly. As Mike's friend remained humble, God was able to promote him. He became a testimony of God's faithfulness to him and to others.

It's imperative that we remain humble in God's presence. Humility brings wisdom, but also the overflow of the supernatural power of God. It's only tapping into our Source that allows us to make any impact for His kingdom.

> Our lives are to exemplify God's magnificence so that others see a visible demonstration of an invisible God.

Lead with a Servant's Heart

The supernatural impact that God wants flowing from us comes from a life of radical humility and radical service. When Jesus served His disciples by washing their feet, this struck them as extremely odd (Jn. 13:1-17). Leaders weren't supposed to do menial tasks. Their minds were stuck in worldly mentalities of position. Before this, they even argued who among them would be the greatest (Lk. 9:46). So, when Jesus came to Peter, Peter said, *"You shall never wash my feet!"* If Jesus, the disciples' leader and teacher, didn't show them this example, they wouldn't have any part with Him. They were called to follow Jesus' example by partnering with Him to build the kingdom.

God's glory is shown as we humble ourselves in our service to others. Now, serving from a religious mindset can elicit a false humility because serving is just something we're *supposed* to do—there's no heart or godly motivation. Or we may find our identity in what we do for the kingdom. We may even falsely think that our service will automatically open doors for God's blessings or favor, and approval from others. God wants us to let go of faulty thinking or our need for external validation. Instead, we're to find identity in obedience and humility.

Service is about attitude; it's about following the heart of Jesus.

Service is about attitude; it's about following the heart of Jesus. Leaders that make the greatest impact are leaders whose humbled hearts stay submitted to God. They don't parade their position or use it for leverage. They know they belong to God and that is enough. They understand their call and the urgency of the day; so, what the world defines as leadership is far from them. True leadership is fashioned when they tap into the heart and nature of God.

Jesus' life was about bringing people from darkness into light. The disciples eventually understood what the Lord had been showing them and served with the *Servant's* heart. We've been entrusted to do the same. When we lead and serve in humility, God is most glorified!

Finding God's Will

The call to reach a lost world is readily understood, but some people flounder to discern God's individual *will* for their lives. Pride is often a hindrance. We may think God is withholding His plan for our lives because of our sin, or we've been deceived to think religious performance is His perfect will. Other times we just fail to ask God for direction. Pride keeps us stuck leaning on our version of truth. *If any of you lacks wisdom, let him ask God, who gives generously to all without reproach, and it will be given him* (Jas. 1:5). God isn't waiting to scold us for lacking wisdom but is instead waiting to give it: *I will instruct you and teach you in the way you should go; I will counsel you with my eye upon you* (Ps. 32:8).

When we know someone intimately, we can know what they're communicating to us without them speaking a word. This happens between close friends, or with a spouse. We know because we've spent time in that person's presence and understand their nature, their mannerisms. Our intimate relationship with God allows for that kind of knowing. Oftentimes, insight and hidden gifts aren't made known any other way. These can be the greatest keys to divine appointments, provision, and promotion.

God is impassioned to bring revelation!

Another hindrance is that we underestimate personal Bible study. *Your word is a lamp to my feet and a light to my path* (Ps. 119:105). As a lamp, the Word helps us identify what is godly and ungodly. It helps us to unlearn things that have adversely shaped our perceptions. As a path, the Word kickstarts our faith to prophesy things hoped for, to trust that grace is available in an unseen future (Heb. 11:1).

Discovering God's will for your life requires absolute confidence and utter dependence on Him. You may have been asking God repeatedly to reveal His will, but confidence rests on His faithfulness. Believe and act that you have wisdom when you ask. God is impassioned to bring revelation!

Staying Humble in God's Will

Discovering the will of God brings a confidence that we're at the right place, at the right time, doing the right thing. We discover God's will in humility, but humility is required to *stay* in His will. Thankfully, God is always looking out for us!

Proverbs 6:22-23 talks about how wisdom will guide us when we sleep, watch over us while we're awake, and speak to us to get us back onto the right path if we've strayed. This is the abundant wisdom freely given to us when we ask (Jas. 1:5).

Isaiah 30:21 reads: *And your ears shall hear a word behind you, saying, "This is the way, walk in it..."* This verse abounds with the beauty of intimacy. It creates a picture of the nearness of the Father giving divine direction and purpose. Understanding his identity, the child receives and responds, *"Only You, Father, have the words of life!"* Intimacy is where we receive God's best for every decision, big or small.

> Only You, Father, have the words of life!

It's our responsibility to humbly steward God's will. When we don't, it's much like running out of gas. When we get in pride, we risk driving on fumes. We literally feel the car shut down as we try to get off the road—even steering is difficult. Without the car's life-giving fuel, it's impossible to move. Without humility, we don't allow ourselves to stay filled with the life-sustaining wisdom and purposes of God's will. Getting to our destination suffers. However, the Word doesn't say that God leaves the proud—He is always with us. He just loves too much to see us stuck in pride.

Many of our dreams and desires are God-willed but over time, they got warped with our interference or the world's influence. Recognize that God is your rock and fortress, He is the One who leads you for His name's sake (Ps. 31:3). He has chosen and equipped you with His Spirit. Staying in His will produces supernatural fruit that gives witness to a faithful and all-powerful God.

Humility and Integrity

For His name's sake, God helps us stay humble. We cannot bring glory to God unless our character is associated with Christ—to His unwavering integrity. Integrity is our aim. There should be no disconnect between who we are in public and who we are in private.

Reputation, on the other hand, is more about the image that people identify us with. It may not be who we really are, but that doesn't matter to the enemy. When image sets the precedent, the enemy will be sure to connect reputation to the image. Our talent, riches, fame, or influence will rise as the brand others aspire to. Reputation can then become what defines us.

Integrity is attached to the power of God. Proverbs 16:32 says that whoever rules his spirit is mightier than the one who takes a city. Our lives can look put together on the outside, but we can give our emotions or desires rulership. When we don't cultivate integrity, we won't carry a consistent representation of Christ.

> Integrity is attached to the power of God.

We choose what we're going to value. John 12:43 talks about loving the praise of men more than the praise of God. Seeking man's approval turns into a trade-off: *I change my stance; you validate me.* This becomes dangerous territory for the believer because we cannot compromise integrity, we cannot deny truth. Others may see this as spiritual pride, religious hatred, and view our beliefs as irrelevant. God's Word is settled; He doesn't change. We don't follow trends, and we don't exalt the world's standards above the Word.

Proverbs 17:19 says that the one who exalts his gate seeks destruction. Gate refers to position and influence. If we're promoting ourselves or even knocking down doors for place or prominence, we will eventually come to ruin.

We don't have to wonder how we will get from point A to point B. God is the only one to open the right doors; so, let Him.

Humility and Patience

We may not want the spotlight or a reputation that tells the world to follow us, but there are other things we earnestly desire. When the doors we've tried to open slam shut, we lose heart and wonder why blessings aren't abounding. We'll cry to God, highlighting our faithful works: *Haven't I studied and prayed and been committed to service?* Pride is a characteristic of Satan, and our righteous acts don't move God. God's love compels Heaven's movement toward us, but we hinder progress when patience hasn't had the chance to have its perfect work (Jas. 1:4).

Immaturity blocks our sensitivity to the gift and person of the Holy Spirit (Jn. 14:16). God's blessings are indeed available to us, but we must humble ourselves and repent of pride to receive them. Repentance makes room for the Spirit's counsel. Ecclesiastes 3:1 says that there's an appointed time and season for everything. When we humble ourselves to that truth, we see the godly things we desire come at the right time and season of our lives, and most importantly, for God's glory!

> Stop trying to be the Holy Spirit and counsel yourself to move and have your being in your timing.

Waiting on the Lord and trusting God are sister themes. Stop trying to be the Holy Spirit and counsel yourself. *Be assured that the testing of your faith [through experience] produces endurance leading to spiritual maturity, and inner peace* (Jas. 1:3 AMP) The testing is how you stand in trying times. Do you stand for God's truth and timing, or do you want things your way? This is part of maturing in Christ. Endurance brings you to a place where your faith is developed, and you lack nothing—including total dependence on God.

Let me boldly say that if you were to completely defy pride right now, your due season is ready. God has been preparing blessings to manifest in your life, but there are areas you've allowed yourself to tightly hold onto pride. If you'd release it, you'll see God's mighty hand work in your favor!

God is a Jealous God

God will resist pride one hundred percent of the time. We have the choice to keep pride from being our downfall. Free will is evidence of God's undying love for us—He doesn't force us to choose Him, He wants us to choose Him.

The indwelling Spirit is jealous for those He passionately loves and supremely values. When we willfully receive the voice of the world and follow its belief systems, we've flirted like an adulteress who broke devotion from her one true lover. We've chased after idols who have eyes for the temporal and mouths that tout their own wisdom. *Do you not know that friendship with the world is enmity with God?* (Jas. 4:4).

God's resistance should be a call to seek the heart who lavishes grace on the humble (Jas. 4:6). We come with a contrite heart, submitting to God's authority to resist the devil (Jas. 4:7, 8). He trains us to deny ungodliness and worldly passions; to live soberly, self-controlled, and godly in this present age (Tit. 2:12).

While we are in this world, we're not of it (Jn. 15:19). When our hearts understand that we're rightful heirs of God, all selfish, worldly acts that we've participated in make us say, *"This is not who I am. What am I doing? I don't have to respond like the world. I'm called to live differently."* We can take authority over our choices and allow them to be governed by kingdom principles. We can begin to walk with the wisdom that's above this world.

We've flirted like an adultress who broke devotion from her one true lover.

We cannot afford to live life double-minded, with one foot in the kingdom and the other in the world. God is jealous for us to live in the destiny He's called us to. He yearns to reveal Himself through us in His power! This is possible when we humble ourselves to consistently choose Him above all else.

Humility and Behavior

In 25 years of full-time ministry, I've found that when people hold onto pride, they tend to behave in pride. Pride begins with how we see ourselves. When we don't understand identity, external voices will try to define us. If we constantly hear that we're angry, timid, sensitive (or anywhere in between), we internalize those labels, and they eventually determine how we will behave.

As believers, we find our identity in Christ. All His attributes become ours. Now, is our behavior always consistent with those attributes? Unfortunately, no. In Romans 12:3 Paul said, *"For by the grace given to me I say to everyone among you not to think of himself more highly than he ought, but to think with sober judgment...."* To think with sober judgment is to consider the life of Christ—how He made Himself of no reputation (Phil. 2:7). Anytime we elevate our station above others, we invite pride to interfere with our emotions and reactions.

Similarly, Paul addressed the Ephesian church and urged them to walk in a manner worthy of their calling. Simply put, if we've been called to follow Christ, put on Christ! Walk in humility, extending gentleness and patience, bearing with one another lovingly so that unity and peace abound (Eph. 4:1-3). When unity and peace go missing within the church, kingdom-building suffers. We can't effectively reach the lost when pride keeps us high and lofty or offended and defensive.

Simply put, if we've been called to follow Christ, put on Christ!

Paul continued his admonition by telling the Ephesian church to put away things like bitterness, wrath, anger, and to instead put on kindness, tenderheartedness, and forgiveness (4:31-32). God loves us but cannot breathe life into prideful behavior regardless of if we think we have a good argument. *For we are His workmanship, created in Christ Jesus for good works, which God prepared beforehand, that we should walk in them* (Eph. 2:10). Humility opens doors to these good works, to the signs and wonders intended to flow through us. Pride keeps those doors shut.

Humility in Action

The reason our behavior doesn't mirror Christ's is because we're not obedient to the Word. *But be doers of the word, and not hearers only, deceiving yourselves* (Jas. 1:22). Our Bibles may be highlighted, but highlights don't equal obedience! We sow the Word so that our hearts flow with truths that govern our actions. In the intensity of trials or relationships, what's inside of us comes out. What do we readily demonstrate when the heat is on?

First Peter 3:8 (NLT) says to *"keep a humble attitude."* This conveys the idea of *retaining possession of.* Humility is to be guarded wholeheartedly, not easily cast away. A humble attitude seeks the Word for guidance and counsel.

Verse 9 tells us to not repay evil for evil. Pride will have us think that evil demands a response. However, Galatians 2:20 reminds us that we've been crucified with Christ. Dead flesh cannot respond to evil. If our identity is intact, we're not easily wounded. Retaliation is the world's response, not ours!

Dead flesh cannot respond to evil.

There is a resistance that develops when we trust God's Word and anchor ourselves in our identity. This is how we maintain peace (1 Pet. 3:11) because as we turn from evil, we're refusing to let it come near our hearts and emotions. We're not letting it derail us, and in turn, we're strengthened with God's grace to get through the journey.

The Lord watches over those who do right; He's open to their prayers (1 Pet. 3:12). But God resists the proud. We choose how we'll respond. When we stay humble, we'll receive more grace because we're doing the right thing.

If you're in a fiery trial now, don't disqualify yourself by getting into pride. Bring your focus back to the Word and the ministry of the Holy Spirit. Don't let pride deceive you to think you can handle this trial in your own wisdom and strength. Pride is like pouring gasoline on fire. Your situation only gets bigger until it's totally consumed.

Humility and Persecution

To choose humility is to participate in an all-encompassing grace relationship with the Holy Spirit and His Word. Here is where we find strength and courage for every situation—even when confronted with persecution.

No one enjoys being the target of persecution, but as Christians, we're aware that it's inevitable. *Indeed, all who desire to live a godly life in Christ Jesus will be persecuted* (2 Tim. 3:12). Persecution is the malicious response of others when we choose to live godly. Our conduct draws attention to the darkness in others, and darkness doesn't like to be exposed (Jn. 19:20). Persecution is the spirit of antichrist.

When people slander, gossip, reject, or mock us for our faith, it's a confirmation that God's goodness is shining through us. We'll begin to look for ways to bless and pray for others: *Lord, how can I further reveal more of You?* Although these attacks are unwelcomed, we can rejoice (Jas. 1:2, Rom. 12:12) because we're engaged in the work God has called us to and impacting the lives He is pursuing.

Persecution is the malicious response of others when we choose to live godly.

Many of us have never had our lives threatened because of our faith, and therefore, have only imagined how we would respond. The Bible gives many examples of those who were faithful to the end. Their common denominator was God! Strength and courage aren't forged overnight; they develop over consistent time in relationship with God and His Word. When we read the *Fear not* scriptures, we humbly submit to God as our source of strength in the midst of trials.

Persecution will reveal a faith that is genuine. Faith is tested as fire tests and purifies gold. Gold perishes but enduring faith stands, bringing evidence of victory on the day Jesus is revealed (1 Pet. 1:6)! God doesn't bring trials; He only brings life. And greater life comes in the form of reward (Rev. 22:12).

We don't know to what degree or exactly when persecution will come. Our response should be one that stands ready.

Humility to Remain Steadfast

God is unrivaled in wisdom and power. When we apprehend this truth, trials have difficulty messing with our emotions or our faith. God will be our help because we've chosen humility over circumstances; we've obeyed His Word to live godly in this present age (Tit. 2:12).

Humility positions us to be used by God to change the atmosphere because God directs our reactions. *Bless those who persecute you; bless and do not curse them* (Rom. 12:14). By remaining faithful to our call, we deny our feelings and trust God as our vindicator. *"Vengeance is mine, I will repay," says the Lord* (v. 19).

Trials we face aren't always because of our faith. Many times, people attack us because they're just lost and operate from the negative emotions that result from pride. When we don't repay evil for evil, the possibility of dialogue then opens for the Gospel. *But sanctify the Lord God in your hearts, and always be ready to give a defense to everyone who asks you a reason for the hope that is in you...* (1 Pet. 3:15 NKJV).

One time in Russia, there was a situation where my husband Mike and I felt utterly betrayed by two people. Our flesh had the opportunity to rage. We truly needed to depend on God's leading—not only for the problem but for our hearts. Everything eventually turned around for God's glory; and my testimony was that God was an ever-present help! With His counsel, Mike and I remained humble and steadfast to the Word. Our flesh didn't rule over us! *But I* [Jesus] *say to you, Love your enemies and pray for those who persecute you...* (Matt. 5:44).

As the world gets darker, we need to be intentional with God and His Word.

As the world gets darker, we need to be intentional with our relationship with God and His Word. If it wasn't for God, we could have the attitudes of our enemies. If not for His promises, we wouldn't have hope. Trust that His Word is the standard for every decision we make.

Humility and Promotion

Reigning in Humility only leads to promotion! God has awesome things for us, but we have to humbly get out of the way. We can't have a prideful attitude or personal agendas. God is God; He's all-knowing. He hasn't designed or spoken anything that doesn't have purpose. This includes you!

God formed you to be His servant in your mother's womb; and it's through *you* that He'll be glorified (Is. 49:3, 5). This is powerful. We understand that this verse is about Jesus. Yet when God looks at you, He sees Jesus! What you see Jesus do in scripture is available to you too. You carry all the attributes of Christ, and all things are possible to those who believe (Mk. 9:23).

Believe that you've been chosen to demonstrate the magnificence of Christ. Stop looking to the generation

> God hasn't designed or spoken anything that doesn't have purpose. This includes you!

ahead to fulfill this call. Stop taking inventory of all that's behind—what you've been through or what little experience you think you have. These things are not a disqualification for a child of God. God can touch and transform anything you bring to Him. He can make things new and accelerate things for His purposes. He's the God who can do abundantly more than you could ever imagine (Eph. 3:20).

Jesus said, *"Whoever exalts himself will be humbled, and whoever humbles himself will be exalted"* (Matt. 23:12). We tend to exalt ourselves because we crave the recognition of man. Other times we exalt our plans because our true motives don't align with God's plans. Either way, we end up having to maintain the path we've carved out for ourselves; but anything we build in our own wisdom will fall (Prov. 16:18).

You will not receive any promotion or move forward without God's wisdom (Prov. 15:33). Humble yourself, repent, and let God teach you today. There are souls that need Him. God will get you to the right places and to the right people. He's entrusted you with His Gospel; entrust your heart to Him.

Conclusion

The beauty behind a study in humility is that it eventually brings us back to intimacy. Sometimes it's the conviction of just one scripture that motivates us to turn around. 1 Peter 5:5 (NKJV) is key to this study: *God resists the proud, but gives grace to the humble.* I don't believe anyone wants to be on the receiving end of God's resistance. If we have, we just need a good reminder of who God is, who we are, and what we are called to do. We get this refresher course through intimacy.

The truth is, we have access to God's grace. It is part of what came packaged with salvation. However, the grace we receive in humility is what James 4:6 calls **generous** grace. This is power-packed grace continuously flowing toward those with a humble heart, **committed** to the call.

A glorious domino effect happens when we share the Gospel with others—when we're living demonstrations of God's incredible goodness. It is God's goodness that leads others to repentance (Rom. 2:4). God's will is to fill Heaven. Jesus came to seek and save the lost. That passion hasn't changed.

The enemy knows this and that's why he wants us to stay in pride. If we don't reach the people we're supposed to reach, then they cannot reach the people they were supposed to reach, and so on.

We can only reign in humility when we identify the pitfalls that keep us from God's perfect will. I've covered many scriptures in this booklet but encourage you to order my CD album, "Reigning in Humility." It gives a more intensive look at how God exerts His divine influence in our lives.

Call for Prayer

If you need prayer for any reason, you can call our Prayer Line 24 hours a day, seven days a week at 719-635-1111. A trained prayer minister will answer your call and pray with you. Every day, we receive testimonies of healings and other miracles from our Prayer Line, and we are ministering God's nearly-too-good-to-be-true message of the Gospel to more people than ever. So I encourage you to call today!

LIFE FOUNDATIONS

CONTACT INFORMATION

Charis Bible College

800 Gospel Truth Way

Woodland Park, CO 80863

info@charisbiblecollege.org

Helpline Available 24/7: 719-635-1111

CharisBibleCollege.org

Also visit Carrie at: CarriePickett.com